Be safe.

by Katherine Kidd (Author), Sabrina Kent (Illustrator)

Experience Twilight travel guide was created for Twilight fans by Twilight fans who live in the Northwest. We gladly share our knowledge of the area and our love of all things Twilight. We hope that you enjoy your visit and welcome you to share your Twilight experience with us and our readers at experiencetwilight.com.

Contents

Look for our special stamp destinations logo. Be sure to stop in to get your guide book stamped.

From the Author

Road Trip
My daughter Jessica and I are super Twilight fans. For her 19th birthday she wanted to take a mother daughter road trip to all the Twilight movie sets. I was more than happy to oblige. That first trip we went to a bunch of main sets around Portland-- Carver, Kalama, View Point Inn and our favorite: St Helens. Because we also took several shopping detours and had spa time in the hotel we didn't make it up to Forks and a few other remote filming locations, on that trip. We had such a blast! We took 9 trips total that first year, 2009. We went back to some of our favorite places more than once and made it a point to find and see as many locations as possible.

Blog
In preparation for our first trip I had a hard time getting info about all of the filming locations. Information was very scattered and hard to find, especially addresses. I gleaned a lot from newspaper articles and fan pics from locals. Some info was inaccurate and some was so vague that we would just drive around the area and ask people for info. It was a lot of fun. Some of the hardest locations to nail down were the Cullen house and the baseball field, but we got 'em! And we wanted to share them with fellow Twilight fans. So, we started a blog to post all the addresses and asked others to post anything they found.

Book
We received a lot of emails from fellow twilighters requesting all the locations in one printed document that they could carry with them. So, we basically took the info in the blog and turned it into a little paper and staple booklet. In midst of our continued travels we got the idea that it would be cool to talk to people at the Twilight locations and get them to do a "souvenir stamp" in Twilighter's booklets. The Stamp Destinations have been a hit with both Twilight fans and the locations-- they love it! As we got new info and Stamp Destinations we've updated the guide and with each edition we've updated the graphics and now have it available in paperback book on Amazon.com and several stores through out the Northwest.

Shop
Jessica is a Business Communications major and has dreamed of opening a retail space. I've been doing web and graphic design from our home office for over 13 years and now that the kids are older I wanted an office location to work out of. It was absolutely perfect for us to open a Twilight fan store in downtown St Helens-- our dream come true, mother daughter Twilight business.

Now, let me tell you about the shop... Just typing about it I could fan girl squeal. The location is a Twilighter's dream-- near several main locations, across from Jilly's and the building was in Twilight. We offer info to travelers, guided tours, put on large Twilight events and a shop full of all things twilight-- t-shirts, autographed items, jewelry, candles, too many things to name off. You have to come see for yourself. (You can read more about the shop and location in the St Helens section of this guide.)

Why Experience Twilight
The name of our blog was inspired by our travels. The books are awesome. The movie will take your breath away. But there is nothing that compares to personally EXPERIENCING these locations for yourself, especially the movie sets. Words can't accurately describe what it's like to walk where the stars and crew walked, eat what they ate and see in person what you saw on the big screen. Come, EXPERIENCE Twilight.

Fellow Twilighters
We welcome your postcards (to put on our fan wall), your stories (to share with other Twilighters on our blog) and your requests.

EXPERIENCE Twilight
294 S 1st St - St Helens, OR 97051

(503) 396-5488

BOOK TOUR

Forks is located in the heart of the Olympic Peninsula, between the Olympic mountains and the wild ocean beaches, several hours west of Seattle, WA.

Stephenie Meyer chose Forks, WA as the perfect setting for Twilight, a modern day Romeo and Juliet with vampires. These aren't just any regular vampires. Nor is our heroine, Bella, any ordinary girl. Edward Cullen and his vampire family can go out in the day but they avoid sunshine. Forks is smack dab in the heart of the Hoh coastal rain forest – the rainiest, cloudiest location in the continental U.S. It's the perfect hometown for vampires who avoid the sun, but not so perfect for a sun-loving Bella (recently relocated from Phoenix) who's unconditionally and irrevocably in love with her vampire boyfriend, Edward.

If you haven't read Twilight yet, you need to put this guide down and head to your nearest bookstore. It's alright. We don't mind waiting and we'll still be here when you get back. If you've already read Twilight, we don't mind waiting if you want to read it again. We understand, believe me.

Meyer chose Forks based on of a ton of research, but she hadn't actually stepped foot on the Olympic Peninsula until after Twilight was published. Many of the places in the book weren't based on actual locations. Even so, it's amazing how absolutely right on she was about all the details of life on the Olympic Peninsula and Forks, especially because she's a native of the Southwest– a much different (and dryer!) climate.

It didn't take long for the people of Forks to fall in love with Twilight, Stephenie Meyer and Twilight fans. As more and more Twilighters made the pilgrimage to Forks, the locals realized they needed to provide a guide for the area and designate locations to serve as stand-ins for the book's famous Forks settings, like the Swan and Cullen houses and a field where they play vampire-style baseball. Other locations, such as the police station where Bella's father works, and the hospital where Edward's father is a doctor, play their own part by providing picture-worthy props.

The 24-hour road and weather recording is 360.565.3131

FORKS

Forks Chamber of Commerce

LOCATION
1411 S Forks Ave, Forks, WA

ACCESS
Open Mon - Sat 10 – 4, Sun 11 – 4

ADDITIONAL INFO
This wasn't featured in the book, but it should be
 your first stop in Forks. The unofficial headquarters for all things Twilight, Forks Chamber of Commerce is a great place to stop for information, vamp and werewolf merchandise, and especially a picture with Bella's red truck. The people are very friendly and love having Twilighters come through town.

They provide visitors with a self-guided tour map of all the local Twilight inspired locations. They are no longer offering guided tours by appointment.

Souvenirs: Maps, jewelry, bumper stickers and exclusive T-shirts only available at the Forks Chamber of Commerce.

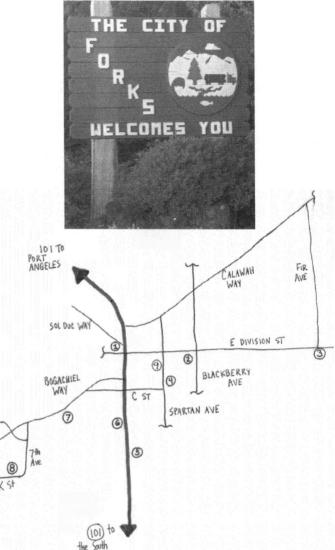

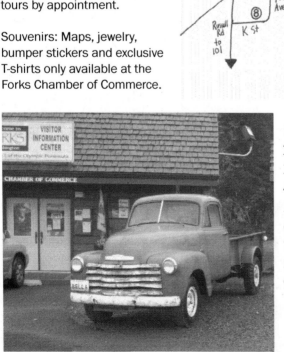

1. Dazzled by Twilight
2. Forks Police Station
3. Cullen House (Miller Tree Inn B&B)
4. Forks High School
5. Forks Chamber of Commerce
6. Forks Outfitters
7. Forks Community Hospital
8. The Swan House
9. Leppell's Flowers & Gifts - "Twilight Central"

Forks Police Station and City Hall

LOCATION
500 E Division St, Forks, WA

ACCESS
Pictures on the grounds

ADDITIONAL INFO
Bella's dad Charlie Swan is the police chief, making the police station an important part of the book. There are parked cruisers outside near which fans can take pictures.

Forks High School

LOCATION
261 S Spartan Ave, Forks, WA

ACCESS
Pictures on the grounds – after school hours and on weekends

ADDITIONAL INFO
Forks High is a main setting in the books, where Bella, Edward, and the rest of the Cullen "kids" go to school. This is where Edward and Bella first meet, where he saves her life, where they go to prom, and where they spend a lot of time getting to know each other at lunch and in between classes. Bella also meets her friends Mike, Angela, Jessica, Ben, Eric, and Tyler here. This is a main setting until Bella and Edward's graduation.

Help save the Forks High School: www.forksforum.com/twilighters

Forks Outfitters

LOCATION
950 S Forks Ave, Forks, WA

ACCESS
Open 8 - 9 every day

ADDITIONAL INFO
This is the Forks local shopping center where you will find the sporting good store where Bella works, and the Thriftway where she does all her grocery shopping. They are very friendly to Twilighters and have Twilight themed cakes, clothing and souvenirs available. For more information, call them at (360) 374-6161.

Cullen House

LOCATION
Miller Tree Inn Bed and Breakfast, 654 E Division St, Forks, WA

ACCESS
Open to the public

ADDITIONAL INFO
Miller Tree Inn Bed and Breakfast has volunteered their 1916 farmhouse inn to represent the Cullen House.

Esme Cullen leaves messages for visitors on a message board by the front door of the inn, and the mailbox bears the Cullen name.

Guests that choose to stay at the Miller Tree Inn are treated to warm hospitality by the Cullen's innkeepers, Bill & Susan (who speak "Twilight"). They love having Twilighters stay with them, and they let you decide which character lives in your choice of rooms. Don't worry, the rooms all have comfortable beds. Bill & Susan know that humans need their sleep!

The Cullen house is the home of Edward Cullen and the rest of his family. It is supposed to be a beautiful and private house hidden deep in the woods on the outskirts of town. Bella spends a lot of time here in all 4 books, especially in the last book, Breaking Dawn.

Souvenirs: Photo of the inn and a message from the Cullens available for purchase.

The Swan House

LOCATION 775 K St, Forks, WA

ACCESS Private - Pictures from the street

ADDITIONAL INFO
This is the house where Bella's parents originally lived when they were married. Charlie is still living there, alone, when Bella moves in with him at the beginning of the story.

The McIrvin family volunteered their two-story Craftsman style house to represent Bella Swan's home—an ideal match to the descriptions in the book. (Please respect the privacy of the home owners and do not trespass. Imagine as many as 100 people a day taking pictures of your house.) Thank you McIrvin family!

Forks Community Hospital

LOCATION
530 Bogachiel Way, Forks, WA

ACCESS
Private – Pictures from the grounds

ADDITIONAL INFO
Dr. Carlisle Cullen works at the Forks Community Hospital. With his 300 years of experience and a vampire's acute senses, he is an excellent doctor. As Charlie says, they are very lucky to have a doctor of his talents in such a small town.

Bella first meets Carlisle in the emergency room after her near deadly accident that Edward has saved her from. As accident prone as Bella is, you'd think she would spend more time here over the course of the books. But knowing the good doctor so well gives her the advantage of more house calls than trips to the ER.

The hospital also likes Twilight and has a parking spot for Dr. Carlisle Cullen in the parking lot where fans can take pictures.

OTHER FORKS POINTS OF INTEREST

Dazzled by Twilight

LOCATION
11 Forks Ave, Forks, WA
(on the main street)

ACCESS
Generally Open 10-6

ADDITIONAL INFO
Dazzled by Twilight is an all Twilight themed store.
Created by Twilight fans who moved their family to
Forks, WA, this store is a Twilighter's dream! Annette
Root runs the store and has a real heart for fan-created projects. The store carries a wide variety of items, from official Twilight merchandise to fabulous and unique fan creations.
They also have Twilight events for special occasions.

Guided tours are available. For general info call: 360.374.5101 or for tours: 360.374.TOUR (8687)

Leppell's Flowers & Gifts - "Twilight Central"

LOCATION
130 S Spartan Ave, Forks, WA

ACCESS
Open 9-5 Mon - Fri, 10-4 Sat., 10-2 Sun. "If the doors are open, we're Open." For more information, call the store at 360.374.6931

ADDITIONAL INFO
Twilight Central! Leppell's Flowers and Gifts is a Twilighter's dream. The owner, Charlene Cross, and staff are welcoming, friendly and always glad to give directions and share a story. Be sure to ask for one of their Twilight maps and get a stamp in your book.

Exclusive Twilight Merchandise.
Leppell's carries a wide selection of unique Twilight items you can't find anywhere else. They have Twilight and Forks High School scrapbooking supplies, Cullen baseballs and tees, Twilight themed treats, home decor items, vampire bite tattoos, jewelry and too much more to mention. You just need to see it for yourself.

Getting Married in Forks?
Leppell's is Fork's hometown florist with over 50 years of experience. They also have tuxedo rentals. They can help make your special day beautiful.

Leppell's Flowers and Gifts is everything you expect Bella's hometown to be.

PORT ANGELES

Port Angeles is the largest city on the Olympic Peninsula, where locals go for movies and a wide range of stores and services. So, naturally, many scenes from Stephenie Meyer's Twilight Saga take place here. Port Angeles has designated a Chamber of Commerce staffer for all things Twilight.

The town will soon print self-guided tours of Twilight sites. And it's working with other towns to host "Twilight" tours and events across the Olympic Peninsula.

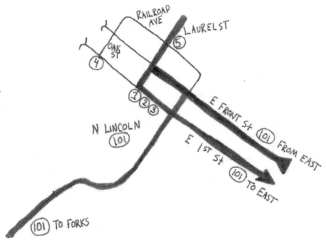

Bella Italia

LOCATION
118 E 1st St, Port Angeles, WA

1. Port Book & News
2. Bella Italia
3. Lincoln Theater
5. Chamber of Commerce / Visitor Center

ACCESS
Open every day at 4

ADDITIONAL INFO
After Bella is almost attacked in Port Angeles and Edward saves her, he takes her out to dinner to calm her nerves and they eat at La Bella Italia. Bella has the mushroom ravioli and drinks two Cokes, at the urging of Edward.

Yes, Stephenie Meyer has eaten at Bella Italia! The downtown restaurant served more than 1,700 orders of mushroom ravioli last year, mostly to "Twilight" fans from all over the world. They accept reservations: 360.457.5442

Dazled by Twilight

LOCATION
135 E 1st St, Port Angeles, WA

ACCESS
Generally Open 10-6

ADDITIONAL INFO
Dazzled by Twilight is an all Twilight themed store. They carry a wide variety of items, from official Twilight merchandise to fabulous and unique fan creations. Guided tours are available. For more info call: 360.374.5101 or for tours: 360.374.TOUR (8687)

Lincoln Theater

LOCATION
132 E 1st St, Port Angeles, WA

ACCESS
Call for shows and times: 360.457.7997

ADDITIONAL INFO
In New Moon Bella goes to the movies twice: once with Jessica and once with Jacob and Mike, right before Jacob turns into a wolf for the first time. The name of theater is not mentioned in the book but there are only two in Port Angeles. The Lincoln Theater is most popular with Twilighters.

Souvenirs: Your ticket stub! Take a break from running around and catch a movie!

Port Book and News

LOCATION
104 E 1st Street, Port Angeles, WA

ACCESS
Open 8 - 8 Mon - Sat, Sun 9 - 5

ADDITIONAL INFO
After Angela and Jessica are done trying on dresses, Bella goes to find a bookstore. In the book she never actually makes it into the store - she just looks in the front. Port Books and News is chosen as this location on the book tour because it is in the same area as Bella Italia and where they would have been shopping.

Souvenirs: Books, bookmarks, pictures

OTHER PORT ANGELES POINTS OF INTEREST

Port Angeles Chamber of Commerce / Visitor Center

LOCATION 121 E Railroad, Port Angeles, WA,

ACCESS Open to the Public

ADDITIONAL INFO
The Chamber runs and staffs the Visitor Center, which is located on the waterfront next to the ferry docks in downtown Port Angeles. 360.452.2363

LA PUSH

Just 12 miles west from Forks, Washington, La Push is home to the Quileute Tribe.
According to their ancient creation story, the Quileutes were changed from wolves to humans by a wandering Transformer. The tribe's lineage stretches back thousands of years to the Ice Age, making them possibly the oldest inhabitants of the Pacific Northwest.

Join the Quileute Tribe every Wednesday night in the Community Center for traditional drumming, songs and dance at 6:00 pm. "It's always Twilight in La Push, WA"

LA PUSH LOCATIONS To go straight to First Beach, turn off 101 onto La Push Rd. Follow it until you hit the coast and you'll see the beach! On the way back, turn left onto Mora Rd soon after crossing the Quillayute River. Then turn right onto Quillayute Rd. The Cemetery will be right when you reach the intersection with Mina Smith Rd.

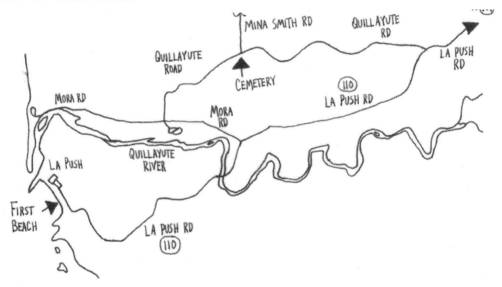

If you want to do this in the opposite order, take La Push Rd from 101 and turn right onto Quillayute Rd after 3 miles. After 4 more miles, you'll be at the junction with Mina Smith Rd and the cemetery. Onward to First Beach: continue on Quillayute Rd for about 3 more miles. Turn left onto Mora Road, and after 2 miles, take a right onto La Push Road. You're about six miles from the beach.

First Beach

LOCATION
La Push, WA

ACCESS
Open to the public / Private

ADDITIONAL INFO
La Push is mentioned in all of the Twilight books. In the first book Mike plans a trip for the group of friends to this beach, during which Bella hears the story of the Cullens from Jacob. In New Moon, La Push is where Bella and Jacob spend a lot of time talking and hanging out, hence "Bella and Jacob's log." Large pieces of trees frequently wash up on the beach, and the pair have important conversations at a distinctive landmark driftwood tree. In the third book Bella and Jacob go to La Push as a place to hang out when Edward brings Bella over. It is an actual beach located in Washington on the Quileute Reservation. However, the movie was filmed at Indian Beach in Oregon.

Baseball Field

LOCATION
Field near the Quillayute Prairie Cemetery,
Corner of Quillayute Rd & Mina Smith Rd, Forks, WA

ACCESS
Open to the public / Private - Pictures from the street / Pictures on the grounds

ADDITIONAL INFO
Anyone up for a game of (Vampire) Baseball? "It's the American pass time!"
In the book this field is a favored spot by the Cullen family – for baseball and large vampire gatherings. It's a safe distance from the town, close to both the reservation and the Cullen house. To play Vampire Baseball, they need a large field far from town and a good thunder storm. That's because Twilight vamps have super speed, super strength, and are as hard as stone. So they need plenty of distance to hit the ball and run, and the thunder helps to mask the sound of the crack of the bat against the ball or even the sound two vampires running into each other. It makes for some fast action baseball! In Eclipse, the Cullens lure newborn vamps to this field. It also plays a major role in the finale of Breaking Dawn.

The field is near the cemetery at the corner of Quillayute Road and Mina Smith Road. Enjoy the field but please be respectful of the cemetery.

MOVIE TOUR

The movie Twilight, directed by Catherine Hardwicke and produced by Summit Pictures, was based on the best selling novel of the same name by Stephenie Meyer. The film stars Kristen Stewart as Bella Swan, a teenage girl who falls in love with vampire Edward Cullen, portrayed by Robert Pattinson. Twilight was released in theaters on November 21, 2008. To date the film has grossed nearly $380 million. This little indy film has become a world-wide sensation!

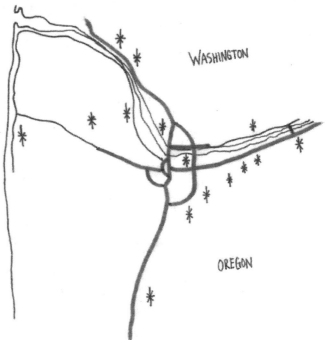

Author Meyer worked closely with screenwriter Melissa Rosenberg and director Catherine Hardwicke and even made a cameo appearance. The producers, directors, cast and crew were all dedicated to keeping the movie as true to the book as possible. They admittedly beefed up a few scenes for the visual effect of the movie but always stayed true to the love story between Bella and Edward.

Most of the actors underwent a transformation of one sort or another to become the character they portrayed. Kristen wore brown contacts, many actors had to bleach their hair and all the vampires wore yellow, black and red contacts. The white face makeup used on the vampires was applied using an ionizer, commonly used in applying Kabuki white face foundation—it sticks to skin and not facial hair, creating a more authentic look.

Even though the book was set in Forks, Washington, most of the filming took place in Oregon. Working out of a base camp in the Portland, Oregon area was easier for Hardwicke to work with a tight budget and time frame. The state of Oregon has no sales tax and has an enhanced film incentive program that offers a rebate of about 17 percent to film makers for money spent within the state—a huge savings. Portland has all the amenities of a city and is centrally located to scenic forest, small towns and the coast— perfect for recreating the scenes from Twilight and convenient for the needs of a large film crew.

Ballet Studio - Yale Laundry Building

LOCATION
800 SE 10th Avenue, Portland, OR

ACCESS
Private business – pictures from the street.

SCENES
The front of the building was shown as the ballet studio when Bella gets out of the cab. (This a wonderful old building in the historic district of Portland.)

PORTLAND, OR

Cullen House

LOCATION
3333 NW Quimby St, Portland, OR

ACCESS
Private residence – pictures from the street ONLY

SCENES
Edward takes Bella home to meet the Cullen family. We see the front of the house when they pull up in Edward's Volvo; the entry area; the kitchen, where the Cullens cook Bella an Italiano meal to welcome her; two sets of stairs; and Edward's room. One of the stairs has graduation joke art on the wall ("We matriculate a lot") and the other has a cross, described in the book, that was made by Carlisle's father in the 1600's.

Edward Cullen: "What did you expect? Coffins, and dungeons and moats?"

Bella: "Um..not the moats."

ADDITIONAL INFO
Summit discovered this house, designed by Skylabs, when it was featured on the cover of Portland Spaces magazine. The home was built for the Hoke family. John Hoke is the VP of Global Footwear Design for Nike. The owners welcome people to take pictures from the street but have asked that fans please respect their private property line and not block neighbors' driveways.

From I-5 take Hwy 30 West. Exit onto NW Vaughn St. Turn left on 26th Ave. Turn right on Thurman St. Turn left on 32nd Ave. Drive to the street's end and park on 33rd Ave.

Madison High School

LOCATION
2735 NE 82nd Ave, Portland, OR

ACCESS
Pictures on grounds – on weekends and after school hours

SCENES
The cafeteria scenes, the science classroom, and some hallway shots.

ADDITIONAL INFO
Some of the cafeteria scenes, like the salad bar, were actually shot back in the studio with a green screen. The on-location shooting happened during spring break in 2008, and a lot of the high school students got to be extras. The spring break weather was great for the kids, but not for the filming crew— the rain you see outside the windows was fake!

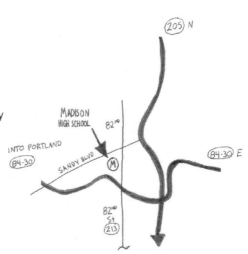

OREGON CITY, OR

Blue Heron Paper Company

LOCATION
419 Main Street, Oregon City, OR

ACCESS
Private business - pictures from the street
ONLY

SCENES
The short scene where the three nomad
vampires stalk and kill the mill guard.

ADDITIONAL INFO
The best place to get pictures for movie
scene locations is in the front of the
building. But if you drive up Hwy 99 (aka
McLoughlin Blvd) through the tunnel, there's an overlook with a great view of the building and the falls that
makes for even better pictures.

Take 205 south from Portland about 15 miles. Exit at #9 (Oregon City). Turn left onto McLoughlin Blvd /
OR-99 E. Go almost a mile, turn right at Main st, and stop. It'll be there on the right.

Clackamas Community College

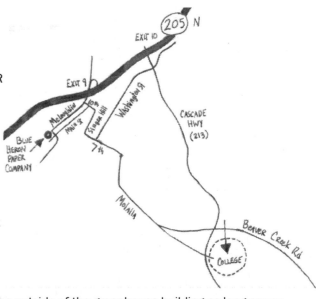

LOCATION 19600 Molalla Ave, Oregon City, OR

ACCESS
Pictures from the parking lot. The campus is
open to the public, but the greenhouse class
isn't (see below).

SCENES
This is the greenhouse that the science class
goes to on their field trip, where we all learn that
"Green is good" and that compost tea is not for
drinking.

ADDITIONAL INFO
The college doesn't care if you take pictures of the outside of the greenhouse building as long as you
don't park your car in someone's designated spot. A few opportunities arise to be able to go inside the
greenhouse, like their Mother's Day plant sale.

Take 205 S from Portland, exit at #10 (Molalla). Turn East onto OR-213 / Washington St and stay on 213
for almost 4 miles. Turn left on Beaver Creek Rd. The college will be about two lights down, on your right.
Enter the campus and the greenhouses and lot will be to your left.

SOUVENIRS: At seasonal events, when available, and photos.

SILVER FALLS PARK, OR

Silver Falls Park

LOCATION
20024 Silver Falls Hwy SE,
Sublimity, OR

ACCESS
Open to the Public

SCENES
Parts of the tree top scenes
when Edward takes Bella high
up into the tree canopy were
filmed at Silver Falls, and so
was the deer chase scene at the opening of the movie. The close up shots of Edward and Bella in the tree canopy, overlooking the river and forest, were shot at Beacon Rock & Cape Horn in WA.

ADDITIONAL INFO
Stunt doubles (Helena Barrett and Paul Darnell) used cable and harness to glide between trees for part of the Edward-Bella scene. Filming was done at the south end of the park, near Parking Lot F and at the Howard Creek Horse Camp.

This park has tent, cabin, and RV camping available, as well as hiking, biking, horse trails, swimming, and

restrooms. About half of the crew camped here during filming. Dogs are allowed on a leash, but be aware that lots of wildlife, including black bear and mountain lions, make Silver Falls their home. What do you want to bet that Edward and Emmett would love to hunt here? ;-)

From the park service: "Please do not pick or dig flowers, ferns, bushes or any other plants. It is also unlawful to harass or capture wild animals."

From I-5, exit at #253 for OR - 22 / OR - 99 (Stayton / Detroit Lake).
Go East for about 5 miles, take exit 7 and turn left onto OR - 214 / Silver Falls Hwy.
Drive about 15 miles, staying on this road, to the park's entrance.

COLUMBIA GORGE, OR

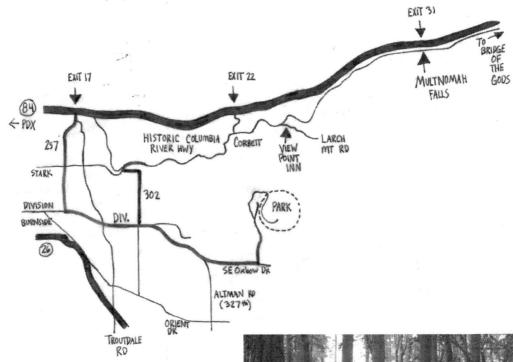

Oxbow Park

LOCATION   3010 SE Oxbow Parkway, Gresham

ACCESS Open to the public /$5 per vehicle fee

SCENES
The "Say it out loud" scene, where Bella tells Edward that she knows he's a vampire.

ADDITIONAL INFO
They used a fog machine here to create the mist, but part of the scene was filmed with a green screen in the studio. If you watch closely, you'll notice that sometimes you can see Edward & Bella's breath when they talk (filmed outside in the cold air) and sometimes you can't (filmed in the studio).

From I-84, take exit 17 (Troutdale) and turn right onto 257th. Go 3 miles and turn left on SE Division St. After 5 more miles, turn left onto Oxbow Parkway.   Then 1.6 miles will take you to the park entrance. The rangers at the gate are usualy good aboutr giving directions. The spot is a few miles in, on the left side, near trail heads D and E. If you've come to the large, gravel parking area on the left, you went just a bit too far but you're close. There's currently tape around the area where they filmed, to protect the vegetation and let it return to its natural state. Note the fallen tree in the background in the picture above– this is almost the exact angle they filmed from.

There are lots of picnic areas, including two tables near the film site. No dogs are allowed because of the wildlife, but there is camping for $15/night, fire pits, restrooms with showers, and RV sites. From the park service: "Plant life and natural resources may not be picked, cut, removed or mutilated."

The View Point Inn

LOCATION
40301 East Larch Mountain Rd., Corbett, OR

ACCESS
Open to the public

SCENES
The Monte Carlo themed prom scenes at the end of the movie.

ADDITIONAL INFO
Outside, they filmed the walkway, gazebo and fountain overlooking the gorge. Inside, they filmed the prom scenes, Victoria looking out of the window in the Roosevelt Room, and the final scene of Victoria walking down the stairs. Walking the grounds and taking pictures can be done any time, but getting inside is a little harder for now. In December 2008 they had a small fire, and the inn is undergoing restorative construction. It's only open for dining and lodging on Saturday and Sunday—call for reservations.

Take I-84 east and exit at #22 for Corbett. Turn right and go up Corbett Hill Road. At the top of the hill, turn left and you'll be on the Historic Columbia River Highway. Drive three miles, then turn right onto Larch Mountain Road. The Inn is the first building on the left.

SOUVENIRS: There are some great ones here! Photo prints of the actors filming, t-shirts, and you can even purchase a personalized brick to be placed on the Twilight Walk of Fame.

Multnomah Falls

LOCATION
50000 E Historic Columbia River Hwy, Corbett, OR

ACCESS
Open to the public

SCENES
Bella and Edward pass in front of the falls as they walk to the baseball field. Other scenes shot here didn't make it into the movie.

ADDITIONAL INFO
You can see the Falls in the background as Bella and Edward are walking to the baseball field. That scene was actually shot directly across the river on private property called The Shire. Scenes of Bella and Edward were shot on the bridge, in front of the Falls but they never made the movie– you may have seen the stills online.

The front of the main building was filmed using green screens, but so far we're unsure what scenes it was used for or if it got cut from the film. The park rangers in the visitor center are very knowledgeable about film sites throughout the Gorge – just cross your fingers for luck and ask, "Do you know anything about the Twilight movie filming?" You never know what fun stories they might share.

Multnomah Falls is the second-tallest year-round waterfall in the nation. The water of the falls drops 620 feet from its origin on Larch Mountain. Hiking trails go up to the bridge in the middle of the falls as well as all the way to the overlook. Work up an appetite? There's a full restaurant at the lodge with a delicious Sunday brunch (we recommend reservations). Espresso and snacks are available outside.

Take I-84 east to exit 31 OR from Corbett, continue along the Historic Columbia River Highway east for about three miles. If you plan to hit the Bridge of the Gods next, you can either follow the Historic Highway east until it connects with I-84 eventually, or go straight back to 84.

SOUVENIRS: The full-service gift shop at the lodge is a Stamp Destination and has wide variety of Oregon and Multnomah Falls themed souvenirs. Take lots of pictures!

Bridge of the Gods

LOCATION
I-84, Exit 44 Cascade Locks, OR / State Route WA-14, Stevenson, WA

ACCESS
Open to the public – Toll Bridge. Fees are Motorcycles, Bicycles, & Pedestrians: $0.50, Small Trailers: $0.50 per axle, Trucks: $1.00 per axle, Dual Wheeled Pick-ups: $2.00, Cars: $1.00.

SCENES
Charlie drives his police cruiser across the bridge, taking Bella home to Forks, in the beginning of the movie.

ADDITIONAL INFO
The best place to take a photo of the bridge is the marine park at 355 Wanapa Street, Cascade Locks, OR. There's only one road in and out of town: Wanapa Street. Just look for the sign to the marine park, about the middle of town, near the soft-serve ice cream stand. (Our family has been stopping at that ice cream stand and the Char Burger Restaurant, in Cascade Locks, since the mid 1970's.)

CARVER, OR

Carver Café

LOCATION 16471 S.E. Highway 224, Damascus, OR

ACCESS Open to the public – closes at 2:00 pm Mon-Fri, 3:00 pm on Sat. & Sun.

SCENES

Charlie and Bella have dinner twice at the Carver Café. The first time Bella meets Waylon, a.k.a. "butt crack Santa", and the waitress reminisces with Charlie and Bella about when Bella was a little girl. The second time we see the café Bella talks to Mike in the parking lot and Mike tells her that he doesn't like her seeing Edward. "I don't like the way he looks at you– like you're something to eat" Mike says. Then it cuts to the inside of the café where we see her royal highness of Twilight, Stephenie Meyer, sitting at the counter with her laptop. The waitress says "Your veggie plate, Stephenie" and then goes to talk with Charlie who's sitting with Bella at their usual table.

When Bella is in her truck, running away from James, being followed by Alice in the Jeep they pass in front of the café. Just before that we see the Jeep following Bella's truck around the corner of a dark road, which also happens to be just beyond the café.

This picture was a prop in the movie.

ADDITIONAL INFO

This is a great, Twilighter-friendly location. The owners are Kris and Sarah. Kris's daughter was in the movie sitting at the counter in the restaurant, and the cook was also seen in the back. Sarah was in it multiple times, once as herself pouring coffee at the counter, and in the scene where the vamps drive by the restaurant she was in the car behind them playing Alice's double. They filmed for 2 days and were also there for an additional 7 days decorating. Sarah said "The man who played Waylon was very fun" and "Stephenie Meyer was so nice" The logo for the café seen in the movie was the original logo. They are willing to take pictures.

Take I-205 S from Portland. Exit at #12A, merge onto Carver Rd / OR 212 / OR 224. The road will split at Alice's Country Market. Branch to the right, staying on 224 (Market Rd). You'll hit Carver about 4.5 miles off 205.

SOUVENIRS: Specialty t-shirts are available, as well as autographs from extras and the owners. Start up a conversation with the locals and bring some stories home!

Bella's table.

The Stone Cliff Inn

LOCATION 17900 S. Clackamas River Drive, Oregon City, OR

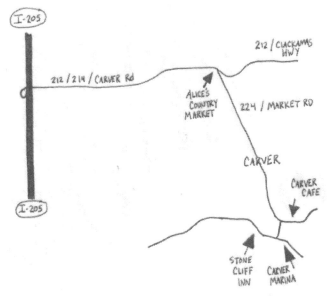

ACCESS Open to the public / pictures from the Street / pictures on grounds from parking lot. You can actually get to where the scene was filmed.

SCENES
When Edward shows Bella that he sparkles. He demonstrates his power by smashing a tree against a rock. The tree Edward is in when he leans down and tells Bella that she is like his own personal brand of heroine. Mossy rocks where Edward confesses his love to Bella. "And so the lion fell in love with the lamb…"

ADDITIONAL INFO
The Inn has signs showing where scenes were filmed. The lion and lamb scene rocks are a little out of the way, behind the tree Edward stood in. The largest in a grouping of rocks still has a large metal hook in it from the harness they used during filming. You should wear casual shoes and watch your step, as this area is rocky and on a bit of a slope.

Scenes when Edward sparkles were added in later by George Lukas' Industrial Light and Magic, using CGI. During filming they experimented with body sparkles and glitter on Rob's double to see what would look best. In the end they used computer animation.

General hours: 11:30am - 8:00pm
Sunday Brunch: 10:00 am - 2:00 pm
(Closed Mondays just for the winter months)
Reservations are recommended - phone: (503) 631-7900

OTHER CARVER POINTS OF INTEREST

Carver Marina

LOCATION
Clackamas River Drive, Carver, OR

ACCESS
Open to the public

ADDITIONAL INFO
Over the bridge in Carver and to the left there is a marina with a large parking lot . This was the crew's base camp while they were in Carver.

KALAMA & LONGVIEW, WA

Kalama High School

LOCATION
548 China Garden Rd, Kalama, WA

ACCESS
Pictures on grounds – see more
details below.

SCENES
The most notable scenes are the
parking lot where Edward saves
Bella from the car accident and
the front of the Forks High School.
The volleyball scenes in the gym,
covered walkway scenes and where
Edward follows Bella into the woods
were shot at Kalama High School.
Some of the less obvious scenes
filmed there were Bella's hospital room and the batting cages.

ADDITIONAL INFO
The crew built Bella's Arizona hospital room set in the wrestling gym for Bella's hospital room. The
basketball gym became Forks gym where they played volleyball. Note in the scene where Edward follows
Bella into the woods, there is a mural on the wall to the left—good for pictures. They also added more trees
to the tree line behind the school. The crew used the school's batting cages in the scene when Renee is
talking to Bella on the phone from Jacksonville. The sign in front was replicated to look like Forks High and
the title above the front door was also replicated. The superintendent's daughter as well as several other
students were extras. Filming took place during spring break (about March 15-25, 2008).

Souvenir stamps and t-shirts are available in the
Superintendent's office all year round. They are
located on the south side of the campus, adja-
cent to the school. Their hours are 7:00 am - 3:30
pm, Monday through Friday.

Twilighters are welcome to take pictures of the
parking lot and stairs during school hours as long
as they yield to school activities. The rest of the
school grounds are available after school hours
and on weekends. We just need to respect that
this is an active school with students.

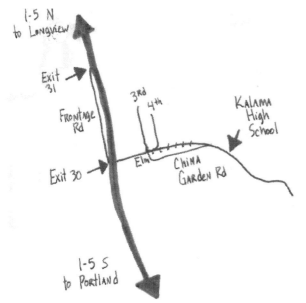

OTHER KALAMA POINT OF INTEREST

Poker Pete's Pizza

LOCATION
164 S 1st St, Kalama, WA

ADDITIONAL INFO
Poker Pete's had to order in extra supplies to provide the cast and crew with several meals over their Spring break shoot. This is a good place to stop for a bite to eat during your Twilight tour.

VANCOUVER, WA

Kadow's Caterpillar Island Marina

LOCATION
10612 NW Lower River Rd, Vancouver, WA

ACCESS
Private business - pictures from the street ONLY.

SCENES
Charlie's friend Waylon is attacked by the nomad vampires while he's working on his boat.

ADDITIONAL INFO
They have no trespassing signs posted, but you get a good view from the street. Parking available across the street.

From I-5, take exit 1C (WA 501 / Mill Plain Blvd) and turn left onto Mill Plain Blvd. Drive about 2 miles, the road turns into tiny NW Lower River Rd. After about

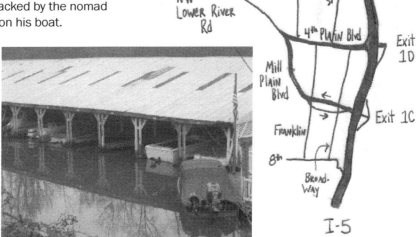

three miles, it'll bend to the left, then jag to the right. Now is a good time to remember all the Twilighters who have come this way before. You are not alone! After almost 6 miles total on this little road, you'll see it on your left. You drive for several miles on a lone, windy road and just about the time you start to wonder if you missed it you'll see it.

Cape Horn Loop

LOCATION
State Route WA-14, near Washougal, WA

ACCESS
Open to the public

SCENES
The close up shots of Edward and Bella in the tree canopy, overlooking the river and forest, were shot here.

ADDITIONAL INFO
As the camera pans around you get a clear view of Beacon Rock and the Columbia River Gorge. Filming took place early April. It rained off and on during filming.
Take SR 14 east to milepost 26.4 (Bus Stop). Take a left onto Salmon Falls Road, then an immediate right into the parking area. The trailhead is across the street on Salmon Falls Road. There is a restroom there. Parking is limited and it's a bit of a hike, but the view is absolutely breath taking.

Baseball Field - The Shire

LOCATION
28852 State Route WA-14, Prindle, WA

ACCESS
Private Property - closed to the public

SCENES
They played Vampire baseball in the field. The nomads appear out of the mist. Bella and Edward walk in front of the Falls (across the river, in the background) on their way to play baseball. The scene when Edward and Bella are sitting on mossy rocks talking about the Cullens being Vegetarians. Lots of good scenes filmed in this one spot.

ADDITIONAL INFO
One of the most popular scenes in Twilight was filmed here: the Vampire Baseball Game. Who can forget Alice's fast pitch, the boom of thunder timed as they hit the ball or as Emmet and Edward collide—all set to Muses' famous song "Supermassive Back Hole". It's a two minute long scene so packed with action, one-liners, charm and energy that words can't adequately do it justice. There was a lot of technical work that went into several of the shots. They make it all look so easy and seamless in the end but in actuality there was a lot of training for the actors, harnesses and riggings, weather issues to overcome and a little CGI for good measure.

Take Washington State Route 14 East, through the Columbia Gorge. The Shire is located at 28852, near the town of Prindle, past Washougal, WA. It isn't well marked, located across from the Skamania County Road Dept Prindle Shop at 28851 SR 14.

The Shire is 75-acres of waterfront property in the heart of the Columbia River Gorge, directly across from Multnomah Falls. It was carefully designed by John Yeon and has sculpted lawns, meadows, wetlands, vista points, river bays, and walking paths. It was donated to the University of Oregon and is used for educational and research purposes like landscape architecture, planning, conservation and preservation. For this reason public tours and private events are not permitted at the Shire.

COASTAL OREGON

Indian Beach

LOCATION
Off Hwy 101 in Ecola State Park, Cannon Beach, OR

ACCESS
Open to the public – dawn to dusk, $3.00 fee at the gate

SCENES
The La Push, First Beach scenes were filmed here, including the van in the parking lot overlooking the beach and Jacob and Bella walking on the beach talking about Quileute legends. That's bull kelp Eric is chasing Angela with–you'll probably spot some yourself.

ADDITIONAL INFO
The ever changing weather of the Northwest provided many challenges for the Summit crew as it would change from a mix of hail, sun to rain during a single scene. Catherine Hardwicke had to be ready with a plan B for each shoot. "We had the backup plan, and the backup plan to the backup plan." says Hardwicke. One such scene was the conversation around the bonfire at La Push, based on the book, was moved to Tyler's van in the parking lot because of weather complications.

Ecola State Park is near the quaint coastal town of Cannon Beach, OR. It has many similar features as the real First Beach on the La Push Reservation in Washington – a variety of colorful smooth stones, weathered logs washed ashore and coastal rock formations.

The road in the park and to the beach is paved in asphalt, long, windy and narrow. Follow it to the end parking lot where the scenes of Bella and friends in the van were filmed. Take the stairs down to the beach and walk to the far south end of the beach where scenes of Bella and Jacob walking were filmed. The scenes with the large rocks were filmed in low tide.

Restrooms are available, as are several picnic tables and some BBQs. On-leash dogs are allowed. Camping

and bonfires prohibited on the beach. There's a hike-in camp 1.5 miles from the Indian Beach trailhead.

Note from the park service: "Plant life and natural resources may not be picked, cut, removed or mutilated."

Take US-26 or US-30 west from Portland to 101 S at the coast. Almost 2 miles south of the US-26 junction you'll see Cannon Beach signs. Exit right onto Fir St., turn right at 5th, and bend right onto Ecola Park Road.

VERNONIA, OR

The whole downtown was transformed to become Forks, WA. Many building signs, including the city hall sign, were covered with signs that said Forks rather than Vernonia. Having been both to Forks and Vernonia, I would say it's a pretty good Oregon counterpart to Forks, WA.

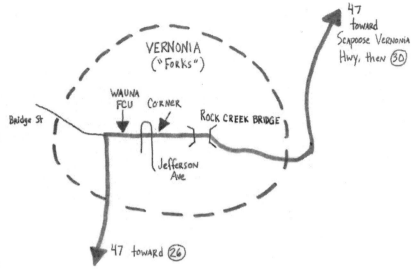

An exact replica of the Welcome to Forks sign was placed just outside Vernonia and that is the sign you see in the movie. The water truck had to come through several times to wet the streets down, to make it look like it had been raining. Driving scenes were shot during the day, using many of the local townsfolk as extras.

Vernonia City Hall is a good place to go for more information. People are very helpful, friendly and love to share their personal stories.

Take US-26 W for about 25 miles after I-405.
Turn right onto OR-47 and drive 15 miles.

Wauna Federal Credit Union

LOCATION
1010 Bridge St, Vernonia, OR

ACCESS
Pictures from the street

SCENES
This bank was transformed into the Forks Police Station, where Edward and Bella stop on their way home from dinner in Port Angeles. Carlisle and Edward talk out front, and Bella has a scene with her father inside.

ADDITIONAL INFO
The filming was all done at night, inside and outside. It was very cold. This was near the end of shooting and the crew was getting worn. They used shrubbery to cover the large sign near the road.

OTHER VERNONIA POINTS OF INTEREST

Rock Creek Bridge in Vernonia

Located in downtown Vernonia, on Bridge St. You see the bridge in the movie when Charlie and Bella first enter Forks, and later as Bella is driving to school in the rain.

Corner of Bridge St and Jefferson

As Bella and Charlie first drive into Forks you see a display of wood carvings to the left and a logging truck crosses the street in front of them. That scene takes place at the corner of Bridge Street and Jefferson. The logging truck is driving on Jefferson, crossing Bridge Street. The wood carvings are displayed in the lot of a tan building that used to be a gas station. Across the street, at 786 Bridge St, you can see a little store called Pretty Gifts and Things – the owner is very friendly and welcoming to Twilighters.

SAINT HELENS, OR

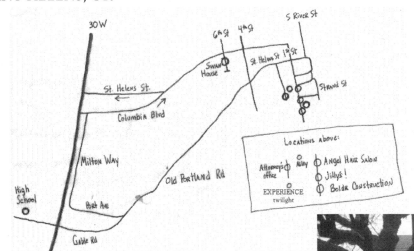

Swan House

LOCATION 184 S 6th St, Saint Helens, OR

ACCESS
This is a private residence - pictures from the street ONLY.

SCENES
The interior and exterior were used as the Swan house,
where Bella lives with her dad, Charlie.
Inside - Kitchen, Bella's bedroom, bathroom, Charlie cleaning his gun in the dinning room, etc.
Outside - Bella's truck and Charlie's cruiser out front, Billy and Charlie in the street, Bella slipping on ice,
etc.

ADDITIONAL INFO
The paved street ends at this house and turns into gravel drive way, though it's not obvious in the movie.
It's easier to park near the bottom of the small hill at Columbia Blvd./ 6th and walk about half a block up
to the house. The house looks just as it did in the movie, very charming and a perfect fit for the description
in the book. It looks freshly painted—it may have been done for the movie, just as they did with some of the
other sets.

Saint Helens High School

LOCATION
2375 Gable Rd, St Helens, OR

ACCESS
Pictures on grounds – after school hours and on weekends

SCENES
Office and hall scenes. Edward playing the piano for Bella.

ADDITIONAL INFO (St. Helens HS Cont.)
The office was transformed into Forks High School office. They filmed scenes of Edward playing the piano at night with lots of back lighting and some fog. Though the music you hear is Carter Burwell's "Bella's Lullaby", Rob was actually playing during the shoot.

Angel Hair Salon

LOCATION
251 S 1st St, Saint Helens, OR

ACCESS
Open to the public

SCENES
This salon was transformed into the Petite Jolie dress shop where Jessica and Angela tried on prom gowns. You could see the court house in the background.

ADDITIONAL INFO
At the time of filming this was Angel Hair Salon. Owner, Brittney Bradford, was very welcoming to Twilight fans. She was an extra in two scenes – one where she was walking on the street and the other where she was sitting with her back to the camera in the Bloated Toad restaurant, with the smiling/sighing guy that is shown when Edward is reading minds and says "cat." Look for her blond hair the next time you watch Twilight. You can also see that scene in the official Twilight Movie Guide Book.

The lovely window paintings of ivy topiaries that can be seen behind Bella in the movie were already on the windows of the salon and may have played a part in Catherine Hardwick choosing this location for the dress shop. You can see the view of the courthouse from the waiting area of the salon, just as it appeared in the movie. (The courthouse and square also appear in Halloweentown.)

Thunderbird and Whale Bookstore - Attorney's Office

LOCATION
260 S 2nd St, Saint Helens, OR

ACCESS
This is a private business – pictures from the street ONLY.

SCENES
Bella inside and in front of Thunderbird & Whale Bookstore.

ADDITIONAL INFO
This is an attorney's office that was transformed into the bookstore in Port Angeles where Bella buys a book about Quileute legends after finding it on the internet in her bedroom.

Alley & Parking Lot

LOCATION
260 S 2nd St, Saint Helens, OR

ACCESS
Open to the public

SCENES
Alley and parking lot outside the bookstore, in Port Angeles, where Edward rescues Bella.

ADDITIONAL INFO
After leaving the Thunderbird & Whale Bookstore, Bella finds herself in a dark, narrow alley and is stalked by a group of men who intend to harm her. They corner her in the parking lot when Edward suddenly appears in his silver Volvo and rescues her from harm. (You'll have to read the "Midnight Sun" to find out what happens to those thugs later.) The "old" murals seen on the buildings behind Bella, in the parking lot, were painted by the movie company on the back side of the 1st Street buildings.

Bloated Toad Restaurant

LOCATION
330 S 1st St, Saint Helens, OR

ACCESS
Currently closed– pictures from street

SCENES
The interior and exterior of the Bloated Toad restaurant, in Port Angeles, where Edward takes Bella for dinner and Edward spills all his secrets.

ADDITIONAL INFO
This building was transformed inside and out to become the Bloated Toad restaurant. In the book the restaurant is called La Bella Italia and is based on a real business in Port Angeles, WA called Bella Italia. For filming all of the windows were covered in black cloth and white Christmas lights were strung over the trellis and the surrounding trees. The Bloated Toad Restaraunt sign was created for the movie. The wood carving of a toad on a log was something the set designer found in the Northwest and added it to the set.

Jilly's

LOCATION
299 S. 1st St., Saint Helens, OR

ACCESS
Open to the Public

ADDITIONAL INFO
Twilight's wardrobe department loved Jilly's and purchased 36 prom dresses and purple fairy wings to decorate the Petite Jolie dress shop scene filmed at the Angel Hair Salon. The cast and crew liked Jilly's and purchased products like capes and sunglasses for their personal use. You can see a Twilight sign Jilly got from the Twilight crew in her front window.

(cont.)

Jilly is a really neat lady! She's very welcoming and chatty, when she's not swamped with customers – it's a busy little place, even on off days. She carries a wide selection of unique clothing, jewelry and accessories. You're sure to find something you can't live without. We bought fairy wings, a skirt, jewelry and a handbag. (I plan to go back and get one of her elegant capes for my birthday.)

SOUVENIRS: Pictures welcome. You have to at least take home a pair of the purple fairy wings, just like in the movie. If you want to really have a fabulous souvenir, get one of Jilly's wild, elegant capes just like some of the cast and crew did!

Klondike Restaurant

LOCATION 71 Cowlitz St., Saint Helens, OR

ACCESS Open to the public

SCENES Interviews were done on the patio area and can be seen on the Blu-ray version of Twilight.

EXPERIENCE twilight

294 S 1st St, Saint Helens, OR   (503) 396-5488

www.EXPERIENCEtwilight.com

EXPERIENCE Twilight

LOCATION
294 S. 1st Street, St Helens, OR

ACCESS
Generally Open 10-5

ADDITIONAL INFO

Our name promises an experience and we intend to deliver. Come to St Helens where you can walk in the footsteps of the stars and crew! Many people don't know that a large portion of Twilight was filmed in little old St Helens, Oregon– just 30 minutes West of Portland, OR. There were nine sets and a lot of background filmed here. The main street in Old Town, where our shop is located, was transformed to become the streets of Port Angeles. The front of our store actually appears in one our favorite scenes. Bella tells Edward to put his seat belt on and he replies with a chuckle "You put your seat belt on." Look for the string of lights around the windows behind Edward—that's us. You've read the books and seen the movies. Come, Experience Twilight!

Experience Twilight has a Twilight Fan Store that provides an experience all it's own. We're glad to help with directions, visitor info or even your special event. We like to take fans pictures for our fan wall. We'll chat with you endlessly about Twilight, if you're in the mood. We have guided walking tours. Best of all, our store is filled with Twilight items from Forks, La Push and around the world. We have t-shirts, decals, jewelry, sparkling vampire venom, rain from Forks, sand from La Push, home decor, suckers, official merchandise, authentic replicas from the movie, exclusive autographed items and more!

To Book a Tour or for more info call: (503) 396-5488